DINOSAUR DIG IT!

W9-BKC-914

SCHOLASTIC

DINOSAUR DIG IT!

Written by Jonathan Kronstadt
Illustrated by Daniel Jankowski and Andrea Morandi
Designed by Bill Henderson

All rights reserved. No part of this publication may be reproduced, or stored in a retrieval system, or transmitted in any form or by any means, electronic, mechanical, photocopying, recording, or otherwise, without written permission of Tangerine Press.

Copyright © 2007 Scholastic Inc.

an imprint of
SCHOLASTIC
www.scholastic.com

Scholastic and Tangerine Press and associated logos are trademarks of Scholastic Inc.
Published by Tangerine Press, an imprint of Scholastic Inc., 557 Broadway; New York, NY 10012

Scholastic Canada
Markham, Ontario

Scholastic
Australia Pty. Ltd
Gosford, NSW

Scholastic New Zealand
Greenmount, Auckland

Scholastic UK
Coventry, Warwickshire

10 9 8 7 6 5 4 3 2 1
ISBN-10: 0-439-92634-3
ISBN-13: 978-439-92634-8

Made in China

Contents

Can You Dig It?

If you love digging in dirt and solving puzzles, you're going to love this book! It's all about paleontology (pA-IE-un-tah-luh-jE), which is how we find out what life was like before there were any people around to write down all that stuff. Like when dinosaurs walked the earth. Getting the dirt on what was going on once people showed up is called archaeology (ar-kE-ah-luh-jE). Keep reading and you'll dig up all sorts of cool facts about how archaeologists and paleontologists piece together the past with the tools of their trade. You'll also learn about four very special dinosaurs, then break open the block in your kit to discover your very own dinosaur fossil! You can even play a cool predator/prey card game with the cards in your kit. So start digging, um, I mean, reading.

What's All This Digging About?

Archaeology and paleontology are the studies of what's left behind. No, not your socks. We're talking about the stuff that people and animals have left behind over millions of years. It may be a pot, a bone, a footprint, a piece of jewelry—just about anything. It may be buried under tons of dirt, or beneath the ocean floor. Whatever it is, if it's from a time when people were around, it's studied by an archaeologist. If it's older than that, it's studied by a paleontologist. These scientists use what they dig up to learn about what was going on way back then. It's amazing what they can figure out from what they find!

It's All Greek to Me

Both the words *archaeology* and *paleontology* come from the Greek word for ancient (that means really, really old) and the Greek word for speech. Makes sense, because what these scientists do is try to dig up stuff that they can learn from, as if the artifacts and fossils were speaking to them about what life was like many years ago.

Kid Finds

Some of the most famous finds have been discovered by kids. In 1879, a nine-year-old girl named Maria was exploring a cave in Spain with her dad when she shined her candle at the ceiling. What she saw turned out to be the oldest works of art ever discovered—cave paintings that were more than 12,000 years old! And in 1947, a boy followed one of the goats he was tending into a cave near the Dead Sea, where he found some bundles that turned out to be parts of the Bible written more than 2,000 years ago. So keep your eyes peeled. You never know what might turn up!

A Puzzling Question

Your favorite puzzle probably has a picture on the box of what it's supposed to look like when it's all put together. But while you start your puzzle knowing the answer, archaeologists and paleontologists start their puzzles with a question. Maybe they want to know whether a particular dinosaur ate meat or plants. Maybe they want to know why a bunch of people left what seemed to be a nice place to live. What they'll do is read as much as they can about whatever it is they're interested in, then figure out what they want to know and where they want to dig.

Breaking up the Earth

When dinosaurs first appeared about 250 million years ago, all the land on Earth was joined together in one huge continent called Pangea. One hundred million years later, a sea began to split Pangea into the continents now known as Asia, Africa, North America, South America, Europe, Australia, and Antarctica. That's why scientists have found fossils from the same kind of dinosaur on different continents. The creatures got separated when the land masses broke apart.

Lots and Lots of Dinosaurs!

Although dinosaurs have been extinct for 65 million years, scientists are constantly learning more and more about them. One paleontology student took a close look at everything we know about the dinosaurs and figured out that there were probably twice as many kinds as we know about now. Good thing those beasts were here before us!

Fabulous Fossils

Fossils are truly amazing! They're an interesting trail of clues that leads back literally billions of years, and scientists couldn't solve the simplest mysteries without them. Fossils are what's left when plants and animals die. They may be the plants or animals themselves, buried in mud or sand that turns to rock over thousands or millions of years and preserves the fossil inside. Or they may be marks the plant or animal left behind. They could be bones, teeth, wood, shells—the harder the fossils are, the better chance they have of sticking around long enough to get discovered.

The First Fossil Find

The first dinosaur fossil was found more than 150 years before anyone used the word "dinosaur." Robert Plot, a museum director, thought the bone found in 1676 in Cornwall, England, was from a giant human. In 1824, William Buckland, a nearby geologist, claimed it was from a giant meat-eating lizard he called megalosaurus. Eighteen years later, Richard Owen, a British zoologist, came up with the term "dinosaurs" to describe the group of extinct reptiles.

Table for Two?
Buckland had a table made out of coprolite, which is fossilized poop!

Older Than Dirt

Fossil hunting has helped scientists figure out just how long things have been living on Earth. Want to guess the age of the oldest fossil ever found? Better bring a lot of zeros, because scientists in Western Australia found some tiny bacteria that are 3.5 billion (that's 3,500,000,000) years old! These bacteria may have been small, but they helped the first plants on Earth produce their own food, which was a really big job.

You don't need as many zeros to "date" the oldest human fossil, but it's a lot older than scientists first thought. In 1967, a team of scientists found human fossils in Ethiopia (in Eastern Africa) that they thought were 130,000 years old. But people who study fossils keep getting better at figuring out how old fossils are, and in 2005, they decided that the Ethiopian fossils were really 195,000 years old!

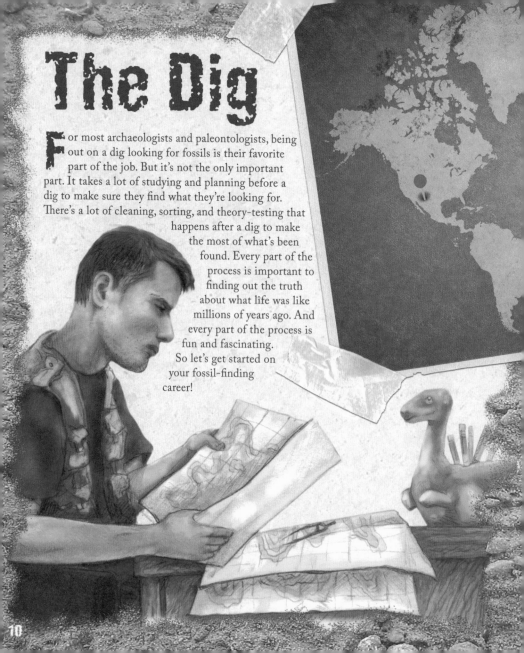

The Dig

For most archaeologists and paleontologists, being out on a dig looking for fossils is their favorite part of the job. But it's not the only important part. It takes a lot of studying and planning before a dig to make sure they find what they're looking for. There's a lot of cleaning, sorting, and theory-testing that happens after a dig to make the most of what's been found. Every part of the process is important to finding out the truth about what life was like millions of years ago. And every part of the process is fun and fascinating. So let's get started on your fossil-finding career!

If Tyrannosaurus rex is the dinosaur you dig the most, aim your shovel at the Western U.S. and Canada. If finding a small, birdlike Oviraptor would make you overjoyed, bring some sunscreen, because you'll be heading to Mongolia's Gobi Desert. If the deadliest dinosaurs are what you desire, rush over to Russia, where Velociraptor fossils have been found. Velociraptors were incredibly fast and had extremely sharp claws. And if you like your dinosaurs with sails on their backs, take a trip to Egypt, where the Spinosaurus strutted its stuff. This colossal carnivore had a big fin that ran across its back and helped it warm up and cool off.

Digging for dinosaurs is cool no matter where you do it. The more you learn before you leave, the more likely it is you'll find something fabulous.

Where to Dig

Where fossil hunters decide to dig depends on a lot of things, like what they want to find, how much time and money they have, even how much space they have to store their fossils. Scientists often get money for digs from the museums or colleges where they work. But let's pretend you're a scientist, preparing for a dig, and you have more than enough money, time, and space for any dig. You need to decide what you want to find!

Maps That Really Rock!

Scientists use geological maps to help them decide where to dig. These maps show what kind of rocks are in a particular area and how old they are. They also help identify the scientists' favorite places to look, like where rocks have been cut open and exposed.

Dressing for a Dig

Fossil hunters who go on digs don't exactly wear uniforms, but there are some key clothes that help them dig longer and do better. The most important thing is staying safe, so they wear sturdy shoes or boots to protect their feet from the rocky roads they'll be traveling. Work gloves, safety goggles, and hard hats or safety helmets are also important items on a fossil hunter's list of things to bring.

Staying warm and dry is right behind staying safe on a scientist's wardrobe wish list. They bring a few light layers—shirts and sweaters—and they always make sure that they have something to keep out water and wind. Any clothing they're not wearing can make a good knee pad for the hours they might spend digging dirt and whacking rocks.

The Well-Dressed Fossil Finder

Ask Before You Dig

Almost all the land on Earth is owned by somebody, so before scientists go digging up somebody's property, it's important to get the property owner's permission. What would you do if you went to play baseball in your backyard and some eager fossil hunters had dug up second base looking for a Gigantosaurus toenail?

Well, first you'd probably tell them that they were wasting their time because Gigantosaurus didn't have toenails. But then you might get mad at them for digging up your ballfield without getting permission. Scientists always ask first.

Tools of the Trade

Dinosaur fossils are special things, so paleontologists need special tools to dig these treasures out of the rocks where the fossils have been for millions of years. A good paleontologist will never go out fossil hunting without:

A geological hammer
Good for breaking rocks apart without pulverizing what's inside.

Brushes
Used to whisk dirt away from fossil finds.

Measuring devices
A ruler and a tape measure to, well, measure stuff!

Tweezers
For tugging free the tiniest of fossils.

Maps
For information about the area where the dig is taking place.

A magnifying glass
For getting a close-up look at fossils.

Trowels
Used for everything from digging and scraping to carrying small fossils.

Containers
To protect precious fossil finds.

Chisels
Used to chip away rock from the fossils.

Notebook and pencil
For jotting down locations, ideas, and anything else that comes up.

Helping Hands

A successful dig takes a successful team. Fossil hunters need lots of help from many people, including:

Geologists, who know all about rocks. Geologists help decide where to dig, and they can tell the age of rocks and fossils.

Draftsmen (and draftswomen), who draw detailed pictures of fossils and rock formations.

Photographers, who take pictures of fossils, rock formations, and anything else worth taking pictures of.

Workers, often students, who dig, chisel, brush, and most importantly, learn.

Specialists, who carefully wrap fossils so they can be moved without breaking or damaging them.

You! There are lots of places where you can dig for dinosaur fossils. Check out page 42 for a list of paleontological possibilities.

Ready, Set, Dig!

OK, so you've got your tools, you've got your team, you've picked your spot—now what? Get digging, that's what! Archaeologists and paleontologists like to explore outcrops, or spots where old rocks have been broken open to reveal the layers inside. This way, they don't have to break the rocks themselves. They also look for places where rivers or railroad tracks have already cut through the rocks. Scientists can look at the rock layers and tell how old the rocks are and what fossils are likely to be found inside.

There are three kinds of rocks in the world:

Metamorphic
(met-a-more-fic), which forms when igneous or sedimentary rock is rearranged by the earth's heat and pressure.

Paleontologist: Species: Dig It!

Sedimentary, which is (sed-a-men-ta-rE), formed when smashed-up rock and seashells settle to the bottom of water and form layers.

Paleontologist: Species: Dig It! Case No:

Igneous (ig-nE-us), which is formed when volcanoes erupt from deep inside the earth.

Paleontologist: Species: Dig It! Case No:

Fossil hunters like sedimentary rock best, because that's where most fossils are found.

Thomas Jefferson: Third President, First Fossil Finder

You may have heard of a guy named Thomas Jefferson, who was the third president of the United States and wrote the Declaration of Independence. What you may not know is that he was also America's first fossil finder! Jefferson dug into a Native American burial mound that was 12 feet (3.6 m) tall on land he owned in Virginia. He wanted to learn more about the people who'd lived there before him. He took lots of notes about how he dug and what he found. He dug so carefully that he was able to clearly see the layers of dirt in the mound and tell when more layers had been added. This method is called stratigraphy, and while Jefferson was doing it in 1784, it was another 150 years before other fossil finders realized what a smart method it was.

It's a Cat. No, It's a Sloth!
One species of prehistoric giant sloth, the Megalonyx jeffersonii, is named in honor of Jefferson, who discovered a fossil of the beast in a cave in West Virginia. Jefferson thought that the fossil might have belonged to a prehistoric giant cat. He named the animal Megalonyx, which means "great claw."

Fossil Found! Now What?

If you're lucky and have done your homework, you or a member of your team will find a fossil bone sticking out of a piece of rock. Now what do you do? First, the fossil finders cover the area with a tent to keep the rain out. Then they carefully begin to chip rock away from the bone until the entire fossil is uncovered. Sometimes it's too risky to get rid of all the rock, so scientists remove a big piece of rock along with the bone and chip away the rest of the rock later. The fossil pieces that stick out are painted with shellac, which is a type of glue that helps keep the fossil from breaking while the scientists work on removing the surrounding rock.

While the fossil hunters are digging, the draftsmen are drawing, the photographers are taking photos, and someone on the team is writing down everything that's important. Each fossil is given a number and measured. Notes are taken on where it was found and what the rock around it looked like (which helps scientists figure out how old the fossil is). Small bones and other fossils are wrapped in tissue paper or cotton and gently packed into small boxes.

Put the Brakes on Big Bone Breaks

If the fossil you find is really big, after jumping up and down for joy, you'll need to protect it so it doesn't break when you try to pick it up. Fossil hunters cover their biggest finds with plaster casts, like the kind people get when they've broken a bone. The scientists then use heavy lifting equipment to gently pick the bone up, and they build wooden frames around it for protection during the trip back to the museum, or wherever it's going.

And You Thought It Took a Long Time to Clean Your Room

Most archaeologists and paleontologists have well-equipped places, called laboratories, where they clean and examine the fossils they find in the field. They have to work very slowly and carefully so they don't break the fragile fossils or put the bones together in the wrong order. Cleaning can mean careful washing with just water or using strong chemicals and acids to eat stubborn rock away from fossils. However it's done, it's an extremely important part of the process, and one that can take quite a while. For example, scientists found pieces of a very old human skull in Africa in 1997, but they didn't know how old it was until six years later. Why? Because it took them that long to clean the pieces, glue them together, and examine them closely enough to figure out that they were 160,000 years old!

Dino Mite!

Fossil hunters have to be gentle when freeing fossils from their rocky homes. Other times they just blast away! That's right— dynamite is sometimes used to blast into rock formations that scientists think are hiding fossils. The trick is knowing exactly how much dynamite to use so they don't smash the fossil and lose the discovery forever. And by the way, this is one technique that should be left to the professionals!

19

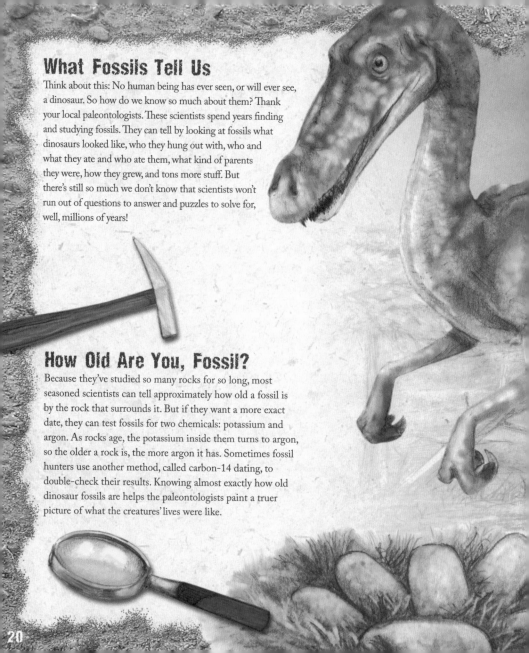

What Fossils Tell Us

Think about this: No human being has ever seen, or will ever see, a dinosaur. So how do we know so much about them? Thank your local paleontologists. These scientists spend years finding and studying fossils. They can tell by looking at fossils what dinosaurs looked like, who they hung out with, who and what they ate and who ate them, what kind of parents they were, how they grew, and tons more stuff. But there's still so much we don't know that scientists won't run out of questions to answer and puzzles to solve for, well, millions of years!

How Old Are You, Fossil?

Because they've studied so many rocks for so long, most seasoned scientists can tell approximately how old a fossil is by the rock that surrounds it. But if they want a more exact date, they can test fossils for two chemicals: potassium and argon. As rocks age, the potassium inside them turns to argon, so the older a rock is, the more argon it has. Sometimes fossil hunters use another method, called carbon-14 dating, to double-check their results. Knowing almost exactly how old dinosaur fossils are helps the paleontologists paint a truer picture of what the creatures' lives were like.

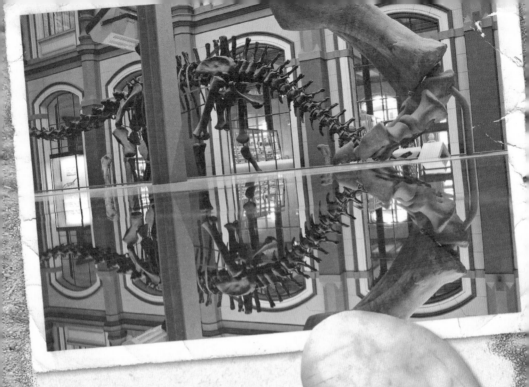

Putting the Puzzle Together

Back at the museum, or in their laboratory, or wherever they take their discoveries, scientists work to figure out what their new fossils mean. They compare the new fossils with old ones, or with fossils that other scientists have found. If there are enough bones from one kind of dinosaur, the scientists may try to put together an entire skeleton. They build a frame that's the same shape as the dinosaur to support the bones as they put them in place. The bones are then wired together, and any missing bones are replaced with plastic ones. Sometimes, there aren't any real bones that have been found for a particular dinosaur. In this case, the skeleton is constructed using all plastic bones. The result is what you may have seen in a museum—a complete dinosaur skeleton.

Prehistoric Poop

Dinosaurs were huge, and they ate enormous amounts of food every day. The result of all that chowing down? You guessed it—literally hundreds of pounds of poop! And believe it or not, a lot of this material, called coprolite, has been fossilized over millions of years, and paleontologists have discovered the stuff in many places around the world. But why would anyone want to study such a thing? There's actually a ton of information that scientists can learn from getting up close and personal with prehistoric poop, such as what the animal ate and how healthy it was. Fortunately, after a few million years underground, even Tyrannosaurus rex poop loses its smell!

The Oldest Dinosaur

Fossil hunters are always digging for new clues to old mysteries. In 1999 paleontologists found what they think are fossils from the first dinosaur to walk the earth—a prosauropod—on the island of Madagascar in the Indian Ocean. They believe the fossils are 230 million years old, and are from small, plant-eating dinosaurs that evolved into a family of huge dinosaurs called sauropods.

Where'd They All Go?

Since dinosaurs aren't here to be studied in person, paleontologists examine dinosaur fossils and come up with ideas about what the creatures' lives were like. These ideas are called theories, and there are two main theories about why dinosaurs became extinct. The one most scientists believe is that about 65 million years ago, Earth was hit by a huge asteroid, or space rock, more than five miles (8 km) wide. The impact caused a giant cloud of dust to cover the earth for years, blocking out all sunlight and killing plants and animals. Another theory is that the weather on Earth changed over time and the dinosaurs just couldn't adapt fast enough to survive.

First Dino Eggs, Then Dino Legs

Dinosaur babies came from dinosaur eggs that dinosaur mommies laid in dinosaur nests. But they weren't up in trees like birds' nests. They were usually dug into sand or mud. The first dinosaur egg fossils ever found were also the biggest. Hypselosaurus eggs, about the size of a football and weighing seven pounds (3 kg), were found in France in 1869. Some dinosaurs laid their eggs and kept on moving. Others, like Maiasauras, took care of their babies. Paleontologists know this because they found adult Maisaura fossils right next to Maisaura babies and eggs.

Dinosaur Dental Dynamos
Dentists are probably glad that Hadrosaurs are extinct. These duck-billed dinosaurs had as many as 1,200 teeth in their jaws, which made them about the most successful plant-eaters ever. No wonder there were so many of them—before that whole extinction thing happened.

The Beginning of the Universe

A timeline is way of marking the most important events in the history of something—in this case, our universe! Here's a peek at what happened when, and who was around to see it happen:

YEARS AGO	
15 billion	The universe is born.
4.5 billion	Earth becomes, well, Earth!
3.5 billion	First signs of life on Earth—bacteria living in sea water.
570 million	The Paleozoic Era begins, and little, hard-shelled animals called trilobites rule the seas.
438 million	First land animals appear in the form of insects, scorpions, and spiders. The first fish with jaws swim the seas.
300 million	Reptiles that lay eggs appear. Some seem like birds, others like mammals.
245 million	The biggest extinction ever, as 95 percent of the world's animal species are wiped out. There are lots of theories about what happened, but nobody knows for sure.
230 million	First dinosaurs appear.
208 million	The Jurassic Period begins, and dinosaurs rule the earth. The first birds take flight, and flowering plants bloom.
146 million	The Cretaceous Period begins, and dinosaurs REALLY rule the earth. Never before had there been so many different kinds of dinosaurs.
65 million	Another big extinction, and this time dinosaurs bite the dust. It's so-long-asaurus time.

Fossil Finding Timeline

Now let's take a look at the history of fossil discovery. It may start a bit earlier than you might think:

YEAR	
600 B.C.	Greek philosophers find fishy fossils on land and figure out that the land they live on was once under water. They're right, but nobody will pay much attention to this idea for hundreds of years.
1770	The fossilized bones of a Masosaur are found in Holland, though it isn't until 1795 that French scientist Georges Cuvier will realize they belong to an extinct reptile.
1841	English scientist Richard Owen coins the word dinosaur.
1858	The first nearly complete dinosaur skeleton is found near Haddonfield, New Jersey. American scientist Joseph Leidy names it Hadrosaurus.
1905	American fossil hunter Henry Fairfield Osborn gives Tyrannosaurus rex its name.
1947	American chemist Willard Libby invents carbon-14 dating, which helps fossil hunters do a better job of figuring out how old fossils are.
1956	American scientist M.W. de Laubenfels is the first to suggest that an asteroid hitting the earth is what caused the dinosaurs to become extinct.
1971	Polish and Mongolian paleontologists find skeletons of a Protoceratops and a Velociraptor together in the Gobi Desert. Scientists believe that the dinosaurs were involved in a fight that killed them both.
1993	American fossil hunter J. William Schopf discovers that tiny fossils found in Australia are the oldest ever found—3.5 billion years old!

OWEN

OSBORN

The History of Archaeology

For a look at some human mystery history, check out this timeline:

YEAR	
500 B.C.	King Nabonidus of Babylon digs up the 2,000-year-old city of Ur.
A.D. 1300	The Aztec people of Central America dig for artifacts in the ancient city of Teotihuacan in what is now Mexico. In A.D. 550, it was probably the biggest city in the world, but by A.D. 600 it had been abandoned.
1722	Dutch explorers find huge statues of people on Easter Island in the South Pacific. No one knows who lived there or why they carved these statues, which stand about 13 feet (3.9 m) tall and weigh almost 3,000 pounds (1,360 kg) each.
1790	Nearly 500 years after the Aztecs had their dig in Mexico, a huge Aztec statue is dug up in the middle of Mexico City.
1822	Human bones are found with woolly mammoth bones in Wales, proving that people and mammoths lived at the same time.
1850s	Scottish scientist Henry Rhind spends two years digging up the ancient city of Thebes in Egypt. He's the first fossil hunter to write down the exact location of every find he makes.
1962	Archaeologists on Newfoundland Island find evidence that Vikings reached North America 500 years before Christopher Columbus did.
1967	Archaeologist Richard Leakey finds two human fossil skulls in Ethiopia. They turn out to be 195,000 years old the oldest human fossils ever found.

Fossil Fakes

The history of fossil finding is littered with phonies and fakers. Some were faked to make money, others to make the fakers look good or others look bad. Two of the most famous were the Piltdown Man and the Cardiff Giant. Piltdown Man was faked by British archaeologist Charles Dawson. In 1911, Dawson combined the lower jaw of an ape with the skull of a modern man and somehow convinced most fossil hunters that he'd found the 500,000-year-old "missing link" between apes and humans. It wasn't exposed as a fake until 1953, 37 years after Dawson died.

The Cardiff Giant was a "man" 10 feet (3 m) tall that George Hull had carved and then buried on his cousin's farm in 1869. He did it to fool someone he had argued with over whether or not giants described in the Bible were real. When the "fossil" was dug up, Hull and his cousin charged people money to come see it, then sold it for $37,500. But when the businessmen who bought it put it on display in Syracuse, New York, scientist Othniel Marsh came to see it and declared it a big fake.

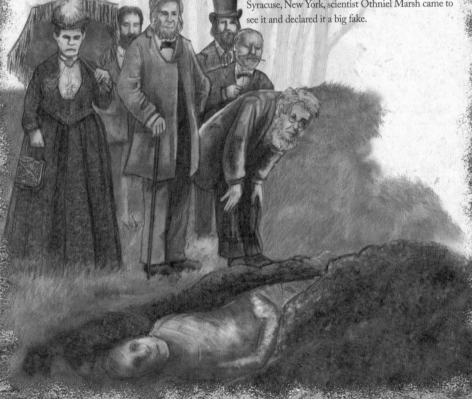

It's Everywhere Under There!

Fossil hunters are dynamite detectives and know where to go to find the finest fossils. Here are some of their favorite spots:

Desert Discoveries

Hot, dry places like deserts keep out the bacteria that can eat fossils out of existence. In 1993, paleontologists found one of the biggest loads of dinosaur fossils ever in the middle of Asia's Gobi Desert. Ancient whale fossils have been found in the desert in Egypt, and trilobites from half a billion years ago have been found in California's Mohave Desert.

Frozen Finds

You know how the food in your freezer never seems to rot? The same is true of fossils. Ice and snow can keep fossils fresh for years. In 1991, two mountain climbers found the 5,000-year-old body of a man sticking out of the ice. His body was so well-preserved that archaeologists could tell what he'd eaten for his last meal. And in 1998, scientists found Hadrosaur fossils in the Antarctic ice, which helped them figure out that there was once a frozen bridge from Antarctica to Australia.

Swampy Stuff

Believe it or not, the well-preserved remains of human beings have been found in various places around the world! We've learned that the natural chemicals in places like peat bogs—swamps filled with dead plants—can preserve human bodies quite well. Scientists have found human remains, which they call "bog people," that have been preserved for about 10,000 years!

Watery Wonders

Fossil hunters love to explore objects that have sunk to the bottom of the ocean. Underwater finds are often fragile, so scientists have to be extra careful. There have been some amazing discoveries made below the surface of the water. Scientists found Heracleion, an entire ancient Egyptian city, that was flooded in the 7th century!

Swim-o-Sauruses?

Dinosaurs didn't live in the water, but some of their close relatives, marine reptiles, did. Picture a dolphin about five times its normal size, and you're close to imagining what an Ichthyosaur was like. Like dolphins, Ichthyosaurs had to come up for air once in a while. Pleiosaurs had four flippers like turtles, but with really long necks so they could breathe air while swimming. Nothosaurs lived on land, but everything they ate came from the sea, so they had to be good swimmers. The longest swimming lizard back then was the Mosasaur, a snake-like air-breather that could grow to be up to 60 feet (18 m) long.

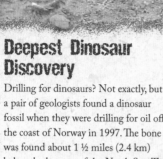

Deepest Dinosaur Discovery

Drilling for dinosaurs? Not exactly, but a pair of geologists found a dinosaur fossil when they were drilling for oil off the coast of Norway in 1997. The bone was found about 1 ½ miles (2.4 km) below the bottom of the North Sea. The geologists turned over their discovery to Norwegian paleontologist Jorn Harald Hurum. It took three years of studying the bone, but the Hurum determined that the fossil was the knucklebone of a Plateosaurus—a big, plant-eating dinosaur that lived about 200 million years ago. It's the deepest dinosaur fossil ever found.

Hey, That's My Bone!

Fossil hunting got competitive in the 1870s in the United States. Two fossil hunters—Othniel Charles Marsh and Edward Drinker Cope—wanted so badly to beat each other to the next new discovery that they each sent spies into the other's camp. They even tried to steal each other's fossils. The two men did manage to find 142 new kinds of dinosaurs between them, but they were also in such a hurry to claim the latest and greatest new finds that they made a lot of mistakes. Cope once put the head of an Elasmosaurus on the wrong end of its body, and Marsh once put the wrong head on the skeleton of an Apatosaurus.

The Day of the Dinosaur

Dinosaurs roamed the earth during the Mesozoic Era, or the "Age of Reptiles," which was 248 million to 65 million years ago—and thankfully, well before human beings! The Mesozoic Era is divided into the Triassic Period, when the first dinosaurs and mammals appeared; the Jurassic Period, which saw many dinosaurs and the first birds; and the Cretaceous Period, which was the heyday for the dinosaurs and also saw the first flowering plants. There were many different types of dinosaurs, from enormous, land-roving meat-eaters that walked on two legs to tiny, speedy winged animals that preferred plants. But despite the differences, one thing is clear—dinosaurs were fascinating creatures! Read on to find out more about four of these amazing animals, then assemble your dinosaur fossil and see if you can figure out which dinosaur you've got!

What Color Were Dinosaurs?

The truth is, we just don't know. Scientists haven't found much dinosaur skin, and what they have found clearly isn't the same color it was when it was on the dinosaur. They believe some dinosaurs were brightly colored to help attract mates or scare away predators. Others may have had colors similar to their surroundings so that they could blend in and hide from animals they wanted to catch and eat or that wanted to eat *them*!

DINOSAUR TIMELINE

DINOSAURS MAMMALS	BIRDS		DINOSAURS EXTINCT	PEOPLE
↓	↓		↓	↓
Triassic Period	Jurassic Period	Cretaceous Period		

├———————————— MESOZOIC ERA ————————————┤ ╫— CENOZOIC ERA —┤

33

Tyrannosaurus rex

"Tyrant Lizard King"

T. rex was one of the biggest beasts ever to walk on two legs. This carnivorous monster lived during the late Cretaceous period, about 85 million to 65 million years ago. Tyrannosaurus rex stood twenty feet (6 m) tall, was 50 feet (15 m) long from tail to snout, and had a head five feet (1.5 m) across. With such a big head, this dinosaur relied on its long, muscular tail to help it keep its balance when it turned suddenly. Tyrannosaurus rex had rough, scaly, bumpy skin, similar to an alligator's. Weighing in at more than 10,000 pounds (4,500 kg), this dinosaur could still move fast enough to catch the other dinosaurs it liked to eat, including Triceratops and Hadrosaurs. And this predator sure liked to eat! T. rex could munch on 500 pounds (225 kg) of meat and bones in a single bite. That's the size of a small cow!

Tons of Teeth

Tyrannosaurus rex had a mouthful of razor-sharp teeth—as many as 60 at a time. The chompers on this carnivore could grow to be almost a foot (.3 m) long! T. rex could bite down with tremendous force too—a single bite could exert four tons worth of pressure.

Paleontologist:　　　Species:　　　Dig It! Case No:

Armed and Dangerous - Sort Of

Tyrannosaurus rex had arms that weren't much bigger than yours! Scientists aren't sure what this dinosaur used its three-foot- (1-m) long arms for. They do know that each arm had two fingers and weren't even long enough to reach the dinosaur's mouth!

Paleontologist:　　　Species:　　　Dig It! Case No:

Huge Head!
The largest Tyrannosaurus rex skull fossil ever found was more than five feet (1.5 m) long and three feet (.9 m) wide—the size of a refrigerator!

Species: Dig It! Case No:

Eye See You!
Tyrannosaurus rex had enormous eyes about the size of a baseball! The eyes faced forward on the front of the dinosaur's head, which allowed it to see how close or how far away an object was.

Paleontologist: Species: Dig It! Case No:

Digging Tyrannosaurus rex

If you live in the western part of the United States, you may be walking where Tyrannosaurus rex walked! Most of the 30 T. rex fossils that have been found were from western states like Utah, Montana, Wyoming, Texas, and South Dakota. The first was found in 1902 in Hell's Creek, Montana, which became a favorite place for fossil hunters searching for remains of this mighty dinosaur. Eighty-eight years later, in South Dakota, paleontologists found the closest thing to an entire Tyrannosaurus rex skeleton. It took six scientists 17 days to get the giant fossil out of the ground, and it took 10 people two years to clean and repair its bones. A Tyrannosaurus rex skeleton has more than 250 total bones, and this one was missing only a foot, one arm, and a few ribs.

Triceratops

"Horrible Three-Horned Face"

Triceratops, which lived about 70 million years ago, was twice as big as a rhinoceros. While Triceratops may have looked scary, it wouldn't have been interested in eating you. This dinosaur was an herbivore, which means it only ate plants—lots and lots of plants! With its huge head and horns three feet (.9 m) long, Triceratops would just knock down big trees to get to the tasty leaves at the top. And imagine this: These giants, who were 30 feet (9 m) long and weighed more than 10,000 pounds (4,500 kg), liked to travel in herds with as many as 1,000 other Triceratops. Just imagine the noise when this group was on the move!

Hard-Headed

Amazingly, many of the Triceratops skulls that have been found are intact. Paleontologists think that the shield on the top of the dinosaur's head helped to protect the animal's skull.

Paleontologist

Train Traveling Dinosaur

The first Triceratops fossil was found in Wyoming in the 1880s. Scientists hauled it up out of its pit by horse-drawn wagon, then sent it on the brand-new Transcontinental Railroad to Washington, D.C., where it's on display at the Smithsonian Institution.

Paleontologist: | Species: | Dig It! Case No:

When in Danger, Attack!

Not many predators would take on a dinosaur as big and fierce-looking as Triceratops. Instead of running away, Triceratops would lower its head and aim its horns at the approaching predator. Only Tyrannosaurus rex was big and strong enough to threaten a full-grown Triceratops.

Paleontologist: | Species: | No:

The Fastest Fossil Picture an ostrich, only with a long tail and no feathers. Now picture it running almost 50 miles per hour (80 km/h), and you've got an idea of the speed of an Ornithomimus, winner of the fastest dinosaur competition. Some scientists believe Ornithomimus was an omnivore, which means that it ate anything it could get its toothless beak on. It was also one of the smartest dinosaurs.

Triceratots?

In 1997, an amateur fossil hunter found what he thought was the dome-shaped skull of a full-grown Pachycephalosaur. But when paleontologist Mark Goodwin saw pictures of the skull and other bones, he knew at once that it was a rare find: a baby Triceratops. The one-year-old dinosaur was just three feet (.9 m) long.

Paleontologist: | Species: | Dig It! Case No:

Pterodactylus

"Winged Finger"

Pterodactylus wasn't a dinosaur, even though it was closely related to dinosaurs and lived at the same time, because dinosaurs didn't have wings. It wasn't a bird, even though it flew like a bird and had hollow bones like a bird, because it didn't have feathers. This creature was actually something all its own— a flying reptile! Pterodactylus was relatively small as compared to other pterodactyls, with a wingspan of up to three feet (.9 m) wide. Some of the other types of pterodactyls had wingspans up to 40 feet (12 m) wide! These flying reptiles soared off cliffs and treetops, gliding down to scoop up fish or any other food they could snatch with their long, pointy beaks and sharp claws. And since the largest Pterodactylus died out 65 million years ago, no bigger animal has ever taken flight.

Far-Flung Flyers
Pterodactylus could fly long distances, thanks to its lightweight wings. It's not surprising, then, that its fossils have been found from Europe to Africa. The first was discovered way back in 1784 in Germany by an Italian naturalist, Alessandro Cellini.

Paleontologist: Species: Dig It! Case No:

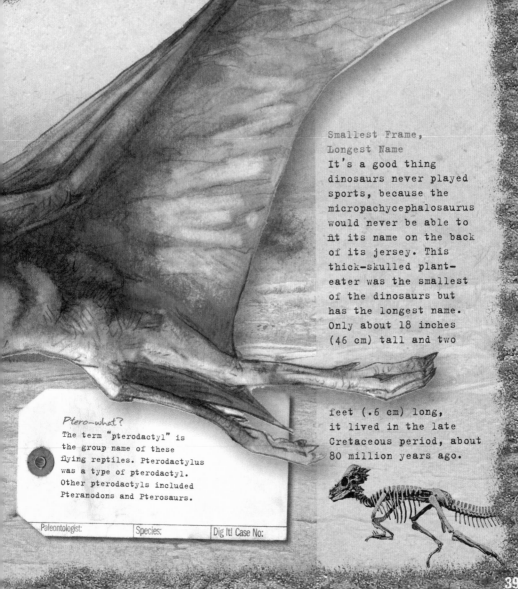

Smallest Frame, Longest Name

It's a good thing dinosaurs never played sports, because the micropachycephalosaurus would never be able to fit its name on the back of its jersey. This thick-skulled plant-eater was the smallest of the dinosaurs but has the longest name. Only about 18 inches (46 cm) tall and two feet (.6 cm) long, it lived in the late Cretaceous period, about 80 million years ago.

Ptero-what?

The term "pterodactyl" is the group name of these flying reptiles. Pterodactylus was a type of pterodactyl. Other pterodactyls included Pteranodons and Pterosaurs.

Paleontologist:	Species:	Dig It! Case No:

Spinosaurus

"Spiny Lizard"

For many years, scientists thought Tyrannosaurus rex was the world's biggest meat-eater, but now they know that Spinosaurus wins the prize for size. This colossal carnivore stretched 55 feet (17 m) from nose to tail and tipped the scales at up to 18,000 pounds (6,800 kg)! And while Spinosaurus loomed large almost 100 million years ago, it wasn't until 2006 that a paleontologist figured out that it was the biggest bone-cruncher on the block, beating out T. rex for the title.

Movie Star

Millions of people learned about Spinosaurus when it was one of the stars of the movie _Jurassic Park III_. One highlight of the movie was a battle between a Spinosaurus and a Tyrannosaurus rex, which could only happen in the movies, because in real life, these two dinosaurs lived millions of years and thousands of miles apart.

Paleontologist:	Species:	Dig It! Case No:

Bombed Away!

Spinosaurus fossils are extremely rare. That's why scientists were incredibly disappointed to learn that the most complete Spinosaurus skeleton in the world was blown up during World War II while on display in a museum in Munich, Germany.

Paleontologist:	Species:	Dig It! Case No:

Sailing Away

The most unusual feature of the Spinosaurus was the huge fin on its back that was shaped like a sail. It may have helped the dinosaur grab heat from the sun to stay warm, attract mates, or scare away enemies.

Paleontologist: Species: Dig It! Ca

That's Fishy

Spinosaurus wasn't your average, everyday meat-eater. In fact, scientists think that Spinosaurus ate a lot of fish, in addition to the smaller dinosaurs that became its dinner.

Paleontologist: Species: Dig It! Case No:

The Biggest Beast

Although paleontologists have found only a few of its bones, they believe that Argentinosaurus was the biggest dinosaur ever. They figured out what the whole dinosaur would look like from bits and pieces of its skeleton. They think Argentinosaurus was 70 feet (21 m) tall and tipped the scales at 100 tons (90 metric tons)!

Keep on Digging!

Hopefully you've learned a lot of great info about digs and dinosaurs in this book. Maybe you're eager to take your tools and tips out into the field (or your backyard) and possibly make some dynamic discoveries. But remember this: A good fossil hunter is a well-read, well-prepared fossil hunter. So keep reading about whatever fossil-finding stuff you like best. Go to your local science or natural history museum and see what kinds of exhibits are there. Take a trip to your local library and check out more books about dinosaurs and fossils. There's a whole prehistoric world out there just waiting to be discovered!

D I Y (Dig It Yourself)

If you're dreaming of digging and really want to get your hands dirty, there are lots of places where kids can hunt for fossils just like real paleontologists! Check out the following list.

Dinosaur Journey
The Museum of Western Colorado
Grand Junction, Colorado

Judith River Dinosaur Institute
Malta, Montana

PaleoWorld Research Foundation
Jordan, Montana

Western Paleo Safaris
Laramie, Wyoming

Dinosaur Research Expedition
Havre, Montana

Old Trail Museum
Choteau, Montana

Pioneer Trails Regional Museum
Bowman, North Dakota

Royal Tyrrell Museum
Drumheller, Alberta, Canada

Timescale Adventures Research and Interpretive Center
Bynum, Montana

The Wyoming Dinosaur Center
Thermopolis, Wyoming

Crow Canyon Archaeological Center
Cortez, Colorado

The Center for American Anthropology
Kampsville Archaeological Center
Kampsville, Illinois

Fossil Digging Instructions

Your kit came with a digging block that has a mystery dinosaur fossil inside! You should also have a digging tool and a brush. Follow these simple steps to unearth your dinosaur. Then check out the pictures on the next page to see which dinosaur you got.

You Need From Your Kit:

Large sheet of white paper

Digging block

Digging tool

Brush

Make sure you're wearing an old shirt before you start digging. Things could get a little messy!

What You Do:

Spread the paper out on a flat surface, and place the block in the center of the paper.

Using the digging tool, gently scrape away the clay. When you see an object through the clay, continue digging very carefully. Remove all the clay from around the object before taking it out of the block. Keep digging until you've scraped away all of the clay and are left with the pieces of your dinosaur fossil.

Brush the fossil pieces to get rid of any extra clay. If you need to, you can also wash off the remaining clay with water to get your fossil pieces completely clean.

PTERODACTYLUS

TRICERATOPS

TYRANNOSAURUS REX

SPINOSAURUS

Paleontologist: Species: Dig It! Case No:

If you want to assemble your dinosaur, you'll need to use strong glue. Ask a parent to glue the pieces together for you. NEVER use the glue yourself!

Dinosaur Duels

A Card Game for Two Players

Challenge a friend to a dinosaur duel!
Pit predator against prey to collect the most points and
win the game.

Materials Needed:

Playing cards from your kit

Scorecard (found on p. 48
of your Dig It! book)

Pencil

Paleontologist:	Species:	Dig It! Case

The Cards

There are 18 dinosaur cards and
two wild cards. The dinosaur
cards are grouped by predator's
attacking strength and prey's
ability to defend itself
from attack. The higher the
Predatory Power or Defending
Power, the more points the
dinosaur is worth.

Predators

●100 POINTS

Tyrannosaurus rex
"tyrant lizard king"

When It Lived
85 to 65 million years ago

Height
20 feet (6 m)

Prey

● 90 POINTS

Pentaceratops
"5-horned face"

When It Lived
Late Cretaceous period,
75 to 65 million years ago

Length
26 feet (8 m)

Weight
8 tons (7.2 metric tons)

Diet
herbivorous (plant-eating)

Defenses
large horns and a huge, tough
skull; traveled in groups

Defending Power
High

How to Play

1. Flip a coin to see who goes first.

2. Player #1 shuffles the deck and deals all of the
cards facedown. Each player gets 10 cards, and he
or she should not look at the cards.

3. Players flip over the top card from his or her
deck and places it faceup on the table. See the chart
at the top of the next page to determine which card
wins the dinosaur duels.

4. The player who wins the hand takes both cards
and puts them aside in his or her own win pile.
Players will add up the points at the end of the round.

5. The round ends when
players have no more cards
to play. Players should then add up the
points from the cards in their win piles and record
their scores on the scorecard for Round One. Players
should then play two more rounds, writing down
their total points on the scorecard after each round.

6. At the end of three rounds, players add up their
points from the three rounds played. The winner of
the Dinosaur Duels is the player with the highest
total number of points from all three rounds.

Predators with:	Beat:
High Predatory Power	Medium and low predators
	High, medium, and low prey
Medium Predatory Power	Low predators
	Medium and low prey
Low Predatory Power	Low prey

Prey with:	Beat:
High Defending Power	Medium and low prey
Medium Defending Power	Low prey
Low Defending Power	Nothing!

Asteroid Assault
Crushed and cremated creatures! Some scientists think that the dinosaurs died off when a single enormous asteroid crashed into Earth. When it crashed through the atmosphere and smashed into the ground, many dinosaurs would have crust, many dinosaurs would have disintegrated with the impact, and the rest would have died of cold or starvation after the dust thrown into the air blocked the Sun.

Climate Catastrophe
Dinosaur freeze-out! One dinosaur extinction theory is that erupting volcanoes caused ash to block the Sun and shrinking volcano made winters colder and summers hotter. The cold-blooded dinosaurs probably could have had trouble adapting to the temperature change and died off.

Wild Cards
(no point value)

Asteroid Assault

Climate Catastrophe

A wild card beats all dinosaur cards. When a wild card is thrown, the player who threw it wins the cards just played and puts them in his or her win pile.

If both wild cards are thrown at the same time, it's a MASS EXTINCTION! The round automatically ends. Players tally the points from their win piles, record their scores, and move on to the next round.

Special Situations

The dinosaur with a higher point value wins the duel. If two cards with equal point value are thrown, no one wins the hand. The cards stay faceup on the table, and each player flips another card from his or her deck. The player with the stronger dinosaur this time wins all four of the cards just played and puts them in his or her win pile to be scored later.

What's Next?
See if you and your friends can come up with your own creative ways to play Dinosaur Duels!

Scorecard

	Player 1	Player 2
	_____	_____
Round 1	_____	_____
Round 2	_____	_____
Round 3	_____	_____
TOTAL	_____	_____

	Player 1	Player 2
	_____	_____
Round 1	_____	_____
Round 2	_____	_____
Round 3	_____	_____
TOTAL	_____	_____

	Player 1	Player 2
	_____	_____
Round 1	_____	_____
Round 2	_____	_____
Round 3	_____	_____
TOTAL	_____	_____

	Player 1	Player 2
	_____	_____
Round 1	_____	_____
Round 2	_____	_____
Round 3	_____	_____
TOTAL	_____	_____

	Player 1	Player 2
	_____	_____
Round 1	_____	_____
Round 2	_____	_____
Round 3	_____	_____
TOTAL	_____	_____

	Player 1	Player 2
	_____	_____
Round 1	_____	_____
Round 2	_____	_____
Round 3	_____	_____
TOTAL	_____	_____